STEPHEN ROMER was born in Hertfordshire in 1957 and read English at Cambridge. Since 1981 he has lived in France, where he is Maître de Conférences at Tours University. He has held Visiting Fellowships at Oxford and Cambridge and has taught in the United States. He has published four full collections, including *Yellow Studio* (2008), shortlisted for the T. S. Eliot Prize. He translates widely from the French, and has edited the Faber anthology of *Twentieth-Century French Poems*. Recently he has published translations of Yves Bonnefoy's *The Arrière-pays* (2012) and an anthology of *French Decadent Tales* (2013). Currently he is Royal Literary Fund Fellow at Worcester College, Oxford. He was elected FRSL in 2011.

T0167933

Also by Stephen Romer
from Carcanet Press

POETRY

Yellow Studio · 2008

Tribute · 1998

Plato's Ladder · 1992

Idols · 1986

AS TRANSLATOR

Yves Bonnefoy, *Poems* · 2017

Into the Deep Street: Seven Modern French Poets · 2009

Alain Dugrand, *Trotsky in Mexico* · 1995

SET THY LOVE IN ORDER

New & Selected

Poems

*

STEPHEN ROMER

CARCANET

First published in Great Britain in 2017 by
CARCANET PRESS LTD
Alliance House, 30 Cross Street
Manchester M2 7AQ, UK
www.carcanet.co.uk

A CIP catalogue record for this book is available
from the British Library: ISBN 9781784103767.
Book design: Luke Allan.

The publisher acknowledges financial assistance
from Arts Council England.

CONTENTS

from PLATO'S LADDER

from YELLOW STUDIO

NEW
POEMS

2008–2017

Training the bellows
on a splinter of sparks
one early morning
of poxed snow
a low moon malingering
in blue-haggard light
and every cell recoiling
in the hollow of the year
on a concrete floor,
it seems the whole technique
of staving off the cold,
and loneliness and the rest,
is to find an angle
on the thing, such as
all is provisional, or else
providential, or *there*
but for the grace of God
go I, whatever
it takes to trick the mind
of a resourceful animal
training the bellows
on a splinter of sparks
it can blaze
into irrational happiness
or at least,
it can take the edge off.

THIS KNOWLEDGE

The gardens, bereaved of our mothers
breathe gently under grey in the sadness
of the morning, and tranquilly they overrun
bounds of the former dispensation.

An ash tree trails its fronds
and a deeper than usual
lilac in a recess looks shy but glowering,
young Kore disturbed by the pond

restored to secrecy, and I then torn
by my own survival, and everything wrong
that was upheld by your joy and worrying
being still in this interim upheld

but how soon to ruin, and this knowledge
suddenly that we are forms of matter,
that dangerous edge, and how we are undone,
and how this knowing also, will run its course.

COMFORTLESS

No you shall not leave us comfortless
as comfort might be
sprays of forsythia over stone

and brisk steps on stone flags
going early through the porch
a trim little body

wrapped against the killing wind
as comfort might be
the longer spearhead of light

along the milled flags
at the opening of the door
as comfort might be

withdrawal and ingathering
a warmth among the ashes
at the start of Lent.

rise from the narrow couch
and descend
barefoot on the stone floor

to Lenten fair, the daily reading
picked up, laid down,
meditation,

words like discipline
and rebirth
the bitter changes

the sloughing off,
a fresh encounter
with solitude, old friend

*

a concussed bluetit in the gloved hand
no self-pity, those out there
surviving, those out there

the measure of our impurity
our complacency
our sloth

the channel black granite
interim between worlds
en bateau, there also I pledged

where the herring gulls
crossed, no slack on them
over the wrinkled acres

*

sealed in
the reddened sallows
burnish
the sand and the snow

hackles of ice
raised on her back
sluggish Loire
charrie son troupeau

but even here
in the sallows, underwater,
there is warmth,
goldblock, terracotta,

her hand in mine
the current running
purity of life
henceforth and hereafter

*

fureur contre l'informe

again I must ask
for a heart as constant
as the throbbing
of this ship

and strong
for each new sickening
of the sea
this need in me

being purposeless
and necessary
the starry heavens
the moral law

*

eternity is the sea
with the sun gone away
leaving the world
slategray

on this deep evening
when loneliness
is formidable
and the effort is

to fork myself out
with a hellfork
from warmth
and forgetfulness

to stand on deck
in the crosswinds
to plight my troth
to make amends

*

silence the voices
(they return)
break the images
(they return)

but in the silence
and the blankness

inklings come back
over the frost
memories of purpose
shocks of honesty

they were covered over
they were styed

*

more visible in winter
the tenacity of small birds
the blushful darling
still delights

other men's phrases
lie strewn about

the purification
of the motive
inescapable
endurance

the light is yellow
on the rough wall
and tender
the blue haze

guard her well
o january rose

ONE YEAR

One year on, the shawl is wrapped
soft round my shoulders and you everywhere
no messages since not a one

the vigil the watch and pray I knew not
watch and pray but that night I did
watch and pray for all I could

except you rose to meet my every move
in the looking glass only the fire
saved me from freezing at every move

where you rose to meet me
in the mirror and when I moved my
every move was a wading through time

the red shawl round my shoulders
when I was terrified to take it off again
and fall forever into the ungraspable

without a hand-hold climbed the stairs
the comfort blanket my shroud
and you not leaving the night-light.

Then you cleared your throat
at the end of the passage
this is and is not, you.

THE BARN

The Barn! Was your burden,
we must clean out the barn!
Your burden, and your cross –

but when at last we made a start
you came storming from the house
and told us to stop,

these were sacred things, not to be
disinterred or discarded lightly,
family things we had no right to handle.

Now it is clean, it is swept right through,
and the archive boxed,
and the boxes removed

at Ferragosta, on the eve
of the Assumption; as Catholic Europe
revelled in cracked bells and fireworks

perhaps in our cool northern air
you rose some echelons
being lighter, the barn empty.

APPLES

Guilt for those things
we have left undone
was your *péché mignon,*
even the apples
became a burden;
belatedly then, this note
to you not to worry
if they went unharvested.

Now in the rigours
an orange beak
uncovers them in the snow,
scores of cherubic reds;
you have laid up
for the hungry a feast.

In the little black notebooks
it is always Ash-Wednesday,
create and make in us
new and contrite hearts

runs the Collect, and the preacher
on that Retreat banged on,
the day is far spent, and we are stranded
on the road to Damascus…

In your private collect, you confessed
to the desert in the garden,
to the 'deadness' and the 'emptiness',
and formed your resolution

to sit still, to banish impurities
and dress yourself in Christ,
your peace in His will, and to seek Him
in the faces of strangers,

commending us your family
all the while, into Christ's safe keeping,
for which bless you, while you struggled
with every variant of the modal *must*.

IN THAT HIGH TENT

To the man on the bus
who thrust some tissues in my hand
today I say
thank you, kind sir

I'd weep myself away
or as if I were being wept
by an overriding force
into a salt and mucus stream

every jointure of the journey
a breakage in the body
and every light red
out of Oxford into London

where you shake against the side

*

You know everything
it is written
the sms gaining in urgency

I recite them still
like scripture

Can you come back?...

Come back if you possibly can...

We go on quietly here...

Just grow wings!

The injunction to ecstasy
stays with me
I saw strong white wings

they were *her* wings suddenly
unbroken sheltering

I knew what to do

Take her hand, take her
broken wing and say the Paternoster

as she did for her mother
murmur and response
under her wing
she in his breast

*

ad te veniam

and stumbled from the taxi
hours later
but wings grown
to the blazing vertical city
up to the encampment
of the loved

our curtained tent
on the summit of K3
where the air had rarified
terribly

and they left us alone
tight screened around

your warm hand in
mine
I have not let go
straightened your shawl
stroked your hair
as never in my lifetime
and held your hand

NOT YET

Take this moment aside
from the dailiness of the days

a block of sheer granite fallen:

run your finger on the dressing table glass
to gather a smidgen of dust

the albums I cannot open
the letters I cannot read.

Not yet, I say, not yet,
now is not the time but there will be time
there will one day be time
there will be
presumably
one day
time

A HOMECOMING

Ruhig glänzen indes die silbernen Höhen darüber,
Voll mit Rosen ist schon droben der leuchtende Schnee.
HÖLDERLIN

And then one day the young master returns
from a dark place
and birdsong leads the wanderer in
and the cat yawns and curls again
in the headiness of this instant
the house is fragrant
with woodsmoke and honeysuckle

which is a kind of accomplishment.

Returning from dogma
home to the humane
he lays aside
knapsack, alpenstock and hat,
goes straight to the piano
sits bolt upright and picks out
1 2 3 of the *Wohltemperierte*.

The *Bildungsroman*, his own,
is unopened on the table,
but let it be, let
the elevation last – for it must fall –
a moment longer.

The blue dome is tense, the gods are close.

Everything is possible.

SEEN IN THE ROUND

i.m. Owen Watson, Lexicographer and Potter

Mornings, he shifts his kitchen chair
to face the rising sun, knows about wind-change;
he has not grown into the garden,
he has grown the garden round him
these fifty years, it rose from the thorns
for us to sit beneath a lime.

He declares – *In a minute it will rain* –
and so it proves. Procession
to the handmade interior, stable door,
settled woodsmoke, swept hearth,
electric fittings to raise the hair,
a scattering of cats,

and then the sun again
riding in on the dust motes.
The cats guzzle on his table
– that's the one place, I venture,
my cat is forbidden – he asks me,
gently, *Any particular reason?*

I would have mumbled 'basic hygiene'
but why argue, how argue,
the case with St Francis?
Cups third shelf straight ahead
sugar second to the left spoons
in the middle drawer

and the sooty kettle is on again.
His Citroen van has turned pale blue
as if fired in a glaze of vine-ash;

it grows its own organic lichen.
A gypsy wanted to buy it – what,
I said, buy my treasure?!

To Mary, *ætat* 94,
he gently discourages
a balloon trip, *the landing can be rocky,*
and in any case, my dear,
you'll see the earth from up above
all in good time!

*

Now glowing in the New Year
the badges and the bosses nearly healed,
the organic van written off – I catch him
rounding the corner, a right-angle iron,
passing beneath a swath of peacock
trailing over the pyracantha.

He has a mission for me, the Catholic
readings for Lent, and a volume
of T.E. Hulme, *Oh have you?*
I'd be so grateful… A relief from the Life
of Eric Gill, and all that fiddling about,
I didn't want to read about that!

Also, twelve bitter oranges,
for marmalade. *When tender*
add the sugar and strain in
the pip liquid. Boil till it jellies.
When it wrinkles down a tilted spoon
let it set. Just so.

*

And then in May, sitting out
in the unseasonal heat,
a dark Africa creeps upon his skull.
Behind his deckchair as he talks
comes a Himalayan shriek
the preposterous fantail whirs
with lust revolving
like the Byzantine mechanical,
a green satin breast
to adorn the thrones of tyrants
and catch the attention
of the indifferent female.

What's that? Oh, is he
showing orff again?
... A whole summer reading Pascal
in snatches, then dozing off,
boring at first, but now I have
the rhythm of his thought
– do you know How he believes?
By the Prophets & the Miracles!

The Maker of Encyclopaedias
sits with an empty head,
samadhi, but the Latin tags are there,
spinozimus, and Scotch boughs –
I think it's what I heard – the multiple flowerlets
over the scooped clay.

*

All Souls, yellow poplar leaves
downrain
after *a marvellous summer.*

The talk is of Matthias Goerne
compared to Fischer Dieskau
– the Duke of Mesland slips out quietly
the moment I put on Schubert.
Could you help me
with this gadget? I need to
mute the soprano –
I find I can take just a little
at a time. Could you get me
a laser needle?

We sit in the ingle-nook,
lamp and book and open fire,
this is where I spend the winter,
it's all I need.
He spoke of his father, a rural priest,
a shock of white windswept hair
striding the coastal cliffs
on visits to his flock
between Scarborough and Whitby.
No priest visits me, and the
churches are falling down!
I leave him, preparing apple jelly.

*

January comes round,
he has pruned his roses early.
The only man in the Touraine
sitting out in a deckchair, pruning!

A formal diagnosis, the swellings
are cancerous, but what of that?
Tests to be gone through,
not worth mentioning.

He reads *The Stricken Deer*
with passion, noting, underlining,
and I understand why,
the deeply reclusive
life of Cowper is his own,
the daily round, and caring
for his hares and his hens.
The 'great events' of the times
pass unheard and unrecorded,
they are nothing to the mignonettes
and the little greenhouse
where the poet sits the summer out,
and entire winters by the fire.

I steer him on to Coleridge –
Holmes to Watson, he noted,
when the packet arrived.
A question, what did Coleridge believe?
Pantheism – then, after suffering,
he returned to belief in the Trinity.
H'm, good. He seems satisfied,
and content to delay Volume 2
where the Life gets gloomier.
I've enjoyed growing up again!
… Dressed in three jerseys,
and I have my arms
round the woodstove; a weeping
in one eye, that makes reading
difficult, but otherwise
I'm absolutely fine.
The cold is polar again tonight.

*

His students came for the 90th
and a Ceremonial Firing.
I liked to vary the flame,
now I just shout orders...
A male abdomen, his final work,
confronts me at the kiln-mouth,
My model, a strapping boy,
found a girlfriend in the village
and never came back!

To one side, some little clays
that were lying about
fired for luck:
greenish with the vine glaze,
two mustard pots with lids,
a salt and a pepper.
Obols to travel with him
when he too is laid
in the fallings of soft ash.

Sleepless in the small hours
perched at the uttermost edge
of the bed or standing
in the rank kitchen
mastering the remote, or not,
for Schubert's *Abschied*
over and over and over
Lebet wohl! es muss so sein,
be well, it must be so.

OXFORD

i.m. Micky Sheringham

In the pink (salmon?) and luminous high room
the conversation is of the mot juste

and surely the mot juste must presuppose
something out there to which justice may be done?

What shade exactly of yellow really is it, say,
twines and untwines in the early autumn

(September) sunshine (sunlight)
over the head of my learned interlocutor

who is talking closely of the *pays de cocagne*
and how from wordplay the nevertheless solid artefact

may come into being without atmosphere, how indisputably
the signs agree there arose a rose – or indeed

a braid, twine, plait, mane revolving silently in the light
beyond my interlocutor through the window

uninvented, I'm inventing nothing – romantic throwback! –
this is happening in my life now (then) *because it is (was)*

a twine of lime or is it sycamore? – I cannot see from here –
(could not see from there) – is untwining against All Souls –

and knowing *which* is life or death, I cannot help feeling
(*feeling?!*) – the life or death of this poem.

from

IDOLS

1986

SEA CHANGES

The novices drink and smoke, or stand
on deck, blinded by the rhetoric
of a riding moon with clouds. Our wake
is white, a crumpled parachute
spreading out behind.

Grown used to this journey through the night,
wrapped in a coat, curled on a seat,
I ask only for a heart as constant
as the throbbing of this ship, and strong
for each new sickening of the sea.

A sheet hung out of a window and shaken
on a morning of sunlight and warm bread
will gather such lights into its folds
that it drains the street and all you see
is this radiant flapping thing, until
it is as suddenly withdrawn, as if there
had been nothing but a black window space.
So the intricate green crystal suspended
at the end of an avenue in autumn
dissolves on approach, and each small light
goes out on its blade.
                It changes nothing;
the milk heats in its pan, and sunlight
breaks on the faces of my friends. Only
at times, but more and more, these absences
and a voice: 'that things continue as they were
is thus the more dangerous and terrible'.

ASPECTS OF THIS SICKNESS

All week the skies have moved upon despair
requiring through folds of various grey
my alteration. They will not allow
a staying place, but move continually
to draw me from my strangling circle,
pierce me with the cry of a bird
and loose upon my head the rains
of immediacy. Those effortless
fallings! No willing brings them down
or spirits away despair.
     But one despair
is spirited; it will move
on workable acres, harrow and turn,
in slowness lift, and over a field
of yellow mustard set the grey skies flying.

'I founded my house on meaning, the extreme
that knelt in yellow to the west, or spoke
from a simple twist of light, an arrow
pointing upward on my wall. How I lay
in wait for it, for what it told, and why
the window set it there! To steal a glance
I broke a penance of the eyes. Visible grace
flying in the air, the daily floodings in
and ebbings out of light were signs to be read
richly into, for I knew him by these things.

A residue of dry secrets. Those corrupt
picturings on the prie-dieu. Schoolmen and dust.
There is nothing to see, touch, taste, smell, hear.
I am a bell they left in disrepair
without a tongue. Looking back is my sin...
I have a narrow bed to meet despair,
pen and paper and blood to dare to tell
of a thing that I know. His indifference
is stern mercy. The sleep of the just
is not different from the sleep of the lost.'

COMING BACK

i.m. James Malpas, 1958–2015, amicus dilectus

When the something withdrawn (you cannot tell
exactly what or when) flows back into the blood
and you return from the damned into your own
(where living is at last to be living now
which the damned cannot know); when your beloved
is again beloved, and morning shows a tree
dressed in light, meaning and memory
at peace in its leaves; when your thought is cool
as linen and you go downstairs to receive
a letter from a friend with total recall
who tells you what you were, and you listen
with attention to the rain on the skylight
which tells you what you are;
                                then you know
that nothing is so lost or gone to waste
that it cannot start again; as when you leave
the city for the pulling air and the sea
which turns upon itself and fills you, something
bows you down to the ground, bows you weeping
down to the sand, weeping there and giving thanks.

AN AFTERNOON IN THE PARC MONCEAU

for Paul de Roux

The weather was foreseen, but not the world
in its field, this was not dreamed up.
But there it was, one interwoven place
where the sun poured down and the children
were moving jewels. A poplar unfurled
its shimmering skein, the candles were dancing
in flocks on a chestnut; they danced in measure,
curtsied, kept balance. And between these things
was no division.

Half way through the afternoon a wedding came
in slow procession through the crossing place;
solemn groom, troubled bride, for all of time
stiffly on the grass. But a smiling wind
unloosed them, and blew her long veil back,
and stretched it out and worried it and showed
her face light up, so animate and lovely
her hands nor his nor any hand could tame
the joyous flapping of that veil.

Lovers on the strong breathing ground,
intercede for us, kiss and kiss, obey
the irresistible thing, be tender
as the folded bird with his soft brown eye
who shares your bank of shade, or say
one motionless branch of becoming.
Beyond them in the half-lights, benched and blessed
between columns, the old sat on amazed
as one more summer climbed to its towers.

For the shy young man from the provinces
life began seven floors up.
His days were a spiralling, down
the narrow stairs, past the acid concierge
on sentry duty at the door, and out
into a sunny vertiginous freedom.

That first autumn was a dream of autumn
unreeling along the intricate paths
of city gardens. Waiting for the winds
to bite into his art, he wrote long letters
to his quickly fading parents, figures
on a daguerreotype of the dead.

Plunged beneath green lamps in the library
his dream continued in the submarine sleep
of vacant faces and swaying heads;
desiring nothing more than this,
he took his place for life
on those benches of the blessed.

It happened on an ordinary day,
mid-week, when he was in a corner seat
of his favourite café. He was convalescing,
weightless, letting the steam invade his thought,
forgetting the mountains, the words on vellum,
his body anchored and his blood at work

from watching the shrunken lamplit street
when a woman he had seen before,
a silent neighbour and companion,
poured her wine to the point of overflowing

and kept on pouring in the horrible growing
silence that rose like walls around her.

He knew he must call her, call her back
invisibly. Wearily he climbed his stairs,
through the sickening density of air
and like a swan reentering its element
he steadied his hand and began to write
with a cold eye under the icy lamp.

IN THE CINQUE PORTS

for Eugénie

At the edge of things, in a bungalow
by the sea, a barometer stuck at 'fair'
ignores the manic sky. It is unmoved
by changeable behaviour in the close
society of weathered ladies
at gin and bridge beneath its glass.
They are an angular, slender-legged
breed; and one by one they go missing.

Discreetly, the merciful visits begin
to their silken tents propped on pillows
and end fantastical in memory, in wraps
of white, like Great Aunt Vi, brought home
from crossing the Zambezi to a death bed
somewhere in Hythe. Her thin extended hand
was a beckoning claw, her piping voice
'come close, come closer child' a terror.

Their line is thinning out, a cluster
of feathered hats on the sea front
threatening to fly in a blast of air
that makes a tatter of tailored skirts.
A flapping row, strung out along the wall
that keeps the sea in place, with its light
blue horizon, unshakeably set fair
beyond the churning salt and mire.

NÉNUPHARS, NYMPHÉAS

for David Gascoyne

This the swollen bandaged hands have done
this delivering up to waters
to the lily's yellow air with absolution.

Absence in a cup, glowing on the waters,
signals from a bed of pale island green
to absence's reflection where the hard head falters;

except this heart's white face was seen
shy mouth pressed by the window's cold,
the question what could lilies mean

so drenched in glass, or how unfold
one surface leaf, is diverlike his work,
his downward knowledge all gloom and gold.

THE WELL

Sick of talk, we cycled down the green tunnel
of altering lights to that village where the well

is just an opening in the middle of the road.
There was no one about, and it was good

to splash our foul words off. It's the chain
of what we do not mean, up against the skin,

scoring cuts where there were none... In that village
the water stood so clear I could not gauge

its level until I dipped a finger in.
I tried, and failed, to see how we remain

transparent like that, as if our modest god
who has no tongue could tell. I know there is a flood

that moves with us. That it is in the flood, at swim
from you to me. That it may not have a name.

MAGPIES

There's speech for this only when she's away
and the big-tailed premonitory magpie
keeps his own bad company

creaking through the thick
sky, and no easy talk
will do, and no high talk

of marriage keeping guard
over another's solitude
– this is solitude

and horribly unlike the medium
we sustain through time;
I cannot name

it, lived in not seen
or known
only as a flickering third companion

is known, or by its rupture,
a whirlpool in the running water
that was clear

and went grey with the breath
of being looked at, the ghost of faith
that went in the space of a breath

– and came back, found its way in
like the rain
– but the window wasn't open –

like her then, opening the door
to join this bedraggled bird, changed by her
into two, and possibly three, or four.

COLOURS FOR THOMAS

We lay together under the gold
curtained window where cobalt travelled
in squares up the wall, exact, controlled

by the scheme that closes orange heat
inside a fringe of violet.
Those squares of blue were desolate,

they sucked us dry;
all that afternoon we lay
stranded in our expectancy.

Nothing can alleviate
a sky so taut,
but sit it out

– it will break for sure
into its reconciling colour.
The day is softened at either

end, so we walked at sundown
when the pink clouds brood on the green
leaves. You showed me again

how crimson lives in the emerald grass,
shadow to its central brilliance,
heart of its ecstasy, the changeless

deathlike tone. The end of light
is constant, mixed on every palette
even as we mix against it

with passion and accident and reason.
Under a window lay our newborn son
crowned by a spectrum, the seven strands of vision.

A copy of *Portrait* by her unmade bed...
Embracing in their common hatred

what am I, against the gut alliance
of Catholic Ireland and Catholic France?

But Dedalus, I know you through and through!
We even share a name. Reading you

I sprouted wings and fled. We are both
at an angle to England, travelling south.

Will you, this once, speak for two of us,
direct her simple wilful heart, release

those channels to remorse, possess her mind,
as I come flying humbly on behind?

I doubt you would enter in so far.
What were your ardent ways but a posture

for being in despair. You had the knack
of detaching what you needed from the ache

of merely needing... Her brief, stifled yawn
has frazzled my patchwork wings to the bone.

... I glimpsed you as I fell, you venerable
heartless survivor, flying out of trouble.

REMEDIES

Learn the use of unhappiness, recommended
apostolic Proust on his death bed,

and no emotion will go to waste.
It is a tempting feast,

but I shall not be drawn a second time
to her forcing-house of a room

where I showed my hand too soon,
those premature, acid green

wrinkled chestnut fingers, unexplained
along her street. I shall remain

at liberty to interpret
the ambiguous spirit

of her calling from the blue like this,
which alone is happiness,

a prolonged underglass imagining
for the asthmatic in his scentless spring.

GRAMMAR

I stick to facts and teach the rules of grammar.
Pasts both perfect and simple, the clamour

of auxiliaries, common defective verbs.
Beginners are secure. Nothing disturbs

their present world with its concrete nouns
in place, as I lead them up and down

a serviceable house. Later I teach
the troubling losses of reported speech

in which my present now becomes his then
and what I say he said, without the passion,

as the active verb I saw can soon
decay into the passive, she was seen...

The early blue is my example
of the limpid future simple,

as when we say it will be fine,
before the rapid clouding through the pane,

the change of tense, the spoiling of a life.
Your heart would have responded, if...

There is comfort in tables, and equilibrium
in a corner seat. Aromatic steam

has taken the place of my head,
it might be fumes across a mask of the dead

I have sat so unnaturally still
this last hour, probably with a smile

that I think might even be wisdom
if wise it is we become

from sitting unnaturally still
and letting the intolerable

be changed into an unimportant detail.
I can drink what she drank, inhale

her brand of cigarette,
and it's easy to interpret

the skull contracting against the skin
– any second she might walk in…

Our café is the same. She's as good as here.
There's life in a table and an empty chair.

HIGHER THINGS

I wish I could, like Søren Kierkegaard,
be absolute and let her face recede

until it is an island in the water
he called memory. Nothing impure

could touch his lasting image of Régine.
Only in memory is love immune

from longing to be with her all the time.
He kept a candle burning in each room,

unfinished manuscript on every desk.
I shall need all his courage for the task

of settling firmly to the sublime;
there is only her face to start from.

Books. Can they help? Is it consoling to know
his love had a pattern mine may follow?

'Triumphant progress, Brumaire to Floréal.'
In Paris, too. But he had circumstantial

perks, a Revolution fairly made his name.
To his natural wit we can add the smell of fame.

The months have lost those lovely names and we're back
in the Ancien Régime, she and I, stuck

in somebody's *Amours* at chanson seven.
From here to chanson twelve is hell to heaven

but our game old poet seemed to work his miracle.
Or was he lying, to finish his cycle?

ENTRE CHIEN ET LOUP

for Gilles Ortlieb

Evening is halogen and cobalt, hunger
and nerves, an objectless desire,

jealousy, enthralment, freedom;
small disturbances before the train home.

And the word 'attrition' is the smell
of oxidised sulphur in the tunnel

of disguised pornography.
We are haggard with frustration, and the sky

has gone more wolf than dog in the interim...
I glide into a bar and out of harm.

In the 'Rendezvous des Belges' there's a man
my veering mind does well to rest on;

a man of substance, with his leg braced back
and his elbows on the zinc, a man of stomach

and slow time, savouring a lager
from the flatlands. They are north of here,

flinty plains and market towns, where the sun
at evening is an inflammation

that lasts for hours. The place was home
for Emma Bovary, a flawless boredom

on which her little sulks were lost,
and all her niceties turned to dust.

She was useful as a scarecrow,
an elegant figure in a field of plough

craving *Passion*! *Félicité*! *Délire*!,
a steamy-shrill arrival at the Gare du Nord

where my stick-in-the-mud will take his train.
I watch him check and pocket his change…

Exulting in that huge equilibrium,
I get up when he leaves and follow him.

RESOLVE

With the problem of the jeune fille
the cosmos and my life to reconcile,

I sat down gravely in a neutral bar
to chew the bread of things as they are

and drink the bitter blackest coffee
ever served by Dame Philosophy,

the grey mistress of severities,
keeper of the pincers, ought and is,

that hold us wriggling in our condition.
Be practical, she said. My consolation

is in your ecstasy when you abandon
hope, and there's nothing to be done.

As for the girl, forget her
and start afresh. A minute later

I tried this out: starting now, I am made
anew. Starting now, I shall conclude

this matter, pay my bill and enter life.
Starting now. It cannot be put off.

– One more coffee then. I shall prevail,
resolved at last. There's just a detail:

am I changed or not, if I tell this tale?

SOUTH

Becalmed in a thirsty garden
with a fig tree, I might yet learn

the sybaritic value of forgetfulness,
and how sweet muscat in a glass

embodies wisdom. Or I could emulate
the drier palate

of a Roman prince of pastoral,
have him share my pauper's meal

of bread, tomatoes, olive oil,
fix my bilious fear of alcohol

and ceaseless blue, wrinkle my skin
to Mediterranean

lizard, deftly untangle
this Gordian matter of a girl

and lay it open in the sunlight
with his candour... 'When you're written out

it shows. Call a halt, decant the best
of your intensity and love its taste.

Your vision of the girl will never fade.
It is neither comfort nor vicissitude.'

from

PLATO'S
LADDER

1992

There's a spring-green boat
moored along the Loire,
waterlogged, unmanned,
dreaming in a green bend
of harbouring river...

In a grove of aspens,
a haze of mirrors,
a brushwork of young oaks
with tender leaves
and a chaffinch

you need not think
of violent deaths
now or as they were
hanged like fruit
from the Castle balcony

but of a gentler kind
your back against the planks
eyes up to the green
into which you disappear
sundazzle and shadow

where the little skiff
imperceptibly loosened
grazes the sandy isles
of the braided river
nosing westward to the sea.

ADULT SINGLE

for Patrick McGuinness

As if a diary redeemed the time
I bring it up to date in a solemn

trivial rite, as if the recent past
were mastered like the latest

headlines, as if, once and for all,
I could get things under control

by jotting them down on this hurtling train
and disembark, born again

– but the appetite dies for reforming prose...
Papers fall from our hands, my neighbours

and I succumb
to warmth, myopia, constant rhythm

where fog has blotted out the landscape.
Cradled to sleep

I'm settling like contents in transit,
my head slips further down the seat,

my thought into solipsism, a sealed shell
of privacies, lulled from level

to level down a fault in the ocean floor.
I'm travelling back, through millennia

of evolution to the whiskered fish,
on the black stream of my single wish

to linger in perpetual motion
behind blue windows and the lash of rain.

WORK

When shall we ever begin?
Swept mercilessly clean

there's a billion billion stars
in the skylight, and our chairs

make their strict companionable arc
with the fire. We're ready for work,

it's the moment we've been waiting for.
After a day of trial and error,

triumph and tantrum,
our baby's down and milky calm.

Our stubborn house
is nearly at peace,

as tamed as it ever will be.
We're dosed with tobacco and Irish tea,

there's a wall of books to be read,
hours of encircled lamplight ahead,

cimmerian voices crying to come in.
Now if ever we might begin

when the cold is eerie but it's warm in here
and we sit without moving, drunk on the idea.

THE WORK

for Valérie Rouzeau

Settling to work is like the idea
of Venice, a cutglass Serenissima

flashing in the mind's eye;
or a tract of country

we left unexplored one summer,
the small hills winding away

into the memory of what was to come,
the peace and space and time

we promised ourselves, but drove on
gazing back at the work to be done

receding in the rearview mirror.
The Work itself is always there,

like Ithaca, grown lustrous in postponement,
or Penelope, or what we most want

and best avoid, our tacit destination.
There are passages in Titian

of lapis lazuli, distances
at the end of experience,

cool water, bridges, hills, a landscape
of reconcilement and essential time

where the work might take shape
under our hands, if we could get there,

and recover those we have lost,
from the first to the last,

if we could say *the last*, renouncing
such kisses as may come

or places we never saw, the idea
of Venice among them, banished forever

from our high blue peak of concentration.

CUCARATXA

The present is another country
belonging to children, or the masked fox
zigzagging nose down on the mountain.

What must it take
to compel me into it;
an earthquake

or a herd of deer
stepping briskly down a vertical?
The close, unhurried scrutiny

of nine Egyptian vultures
wheeling out
from a rockface?

The present is the prayer
of the mantis
to paralyse the fly

and the cellular eyes of the fly
are riveted on the present...
There's an aspect of hell –

the protean mind fixed
in a circular system
of its own devising,

sealed from the here and now
in the single shape
of its own despair...

For half an hour
I would inhabit
the greengold body of the grasshopper,

chafing my red hydraulics
for the sake of it,
or punting for dear life in the stream,

sluggish in shadow, galvanised in sun,
chirpy forgetfulness
my only store.

MYTHOLOGIES

I. Temptation

What did the lake god say
in his annunciation
– pulsings of his turquoise body
through the blackness of a pine –

or what did I ascribe to him?
Apollonian light,
mineral tenacities.
Could he not excoriate

those clinging tendrils
that persist in me
of merely organic fibre,
fear, obsession, desire, envy?

Bind me up with granite,
the sapphire gentian at my feet.

II. Painter

for Caroline

You are my Proserpine of summer
knee-deep in the scabious and mallow,

red-eyed from looking in the light,
as if there were grief or fever
in your exacting tribute
to momentary outcrops of yellow,

painting against the time

when rapidly over the rim
of the granite mountain circus

or in the sealed cranium
at noon on the clearest day,

streams a vocabulary of blackness
no sunlight in the lap of the valley
holds at bay.

THE MASTER IN ITALY

His thought is chaste as a eunuch
though not unmoved by the Baroque

Ecclesia di Gesù, a lusty baritone
and an opulent young nun.

Indiscretions! To walk in Rome
without an overcoat, and countenance boredom

as an elegance in the young,
though it isn't quite done

to preen in bar mirrors or recline
in the Pincio for a whole afternoon.

Supreme badinage... but leave him in the evergreen
fatigue of a dusty villa garden

and he rinses his reader
of approximate despair

by weighing the cornices
of actual light, and speaking sentences.

CAUTIONARY TALE

In contemplation at the café,
a dazed young man out of Cavafy,

'the poet nearing his twenty-fifth year'
gone from bankrupt to millionaire

in the small white hours of eros.
He walks into a morning of promise

and sunlight, with a world-including smile,
startled to find business as usual,

and on his body the surplus greatcoat
from the hopeless months, with the torn pocket

where coins disappeared in the lining;
the same body too, not hunching along

this morning though, but cock of the walk,
the lover tolerant of discourteous traffic,

exuding the benevolence
of a man whose work has been praised, once,

in the press... Now he's at his zenith
in the café; but the waiter's brisk cloth

is applied to the next door table,
change is ceaseless and imperceptible,

the world is moving round him in his dream,
but the world is moving on without him.

By now, he has no
single destination, only
a precarious alternative
with time running out...
The early choice
of thrilling guilt
or consoling virtue
has been replaced
by two flaming angels
of recrimination.

He is skinnier
than ever before
and the owner
of several plastic bags
each containing
a forgotten toothbrush.
His books are stored
strategically, according
to unpredictable
laws of access.

He spends hours
in traffic jams,
travelling to a car park
on the hard shoulder
of a suburb, to escape
the agents of bad luck
who are even now
fining his windscreen.
They provide an excuse
to leave quickly in the morning.

He is often in cinemas
and confuses
Liaisons dangereuses with
Fatal Attraction;
he devours novels
none of which quite apply
to his case...
He decides to keep in trim
by reading deconstructive
revelries over the void.

He is importuned
by certain phrases –
Moral Choice or *The New Life*,
The Children or *The Stock of Memory*;
he rehearses them
in the metro
travelling towards evening,
stirred by perfume
and a frank sexuality
pouting on every wall.

Five o'clock
is the blessed hour
after work and before
decisions, the delicate
negotiation
on a public phone.
The first drink.
He walks decidedly
to the *Café de l'Espérance*
elected

among other things
for the waitress.
He comes alongside
the gleaming chrome and asks her
about the tulips.
De la Porte des Lilas...
He recalls it,
a fragrant name
from a remote life.

'Now I must ask it, what is virtue,
our strong lost word, what is its hue,

its honour, is it an end or a beginning
for such as I in my sixtieth spring

when the fluff is blowing in my eyes
and the deadweight lifting gives rise

to absurd lightnesses on wings,
to pods, seedclocks, haze, trumpetings,

the dogstooth violet, bluebell, heartsease?
What can I make of these,

or of the gentian,
distilled by this April rain

on the upper slopes, if not a quality
engendered, like virtue, petals of the sea

in the mind of a landlocked people,
an idea of ascent, a principle

of detachment from the local pain of love...
To climb for wisdom is to move

from the one beloved to the general
and thence—'
                    '—to your "blessed autumnal

calm". You've tried it before. And when you see
blossom from the wild cherry tree

detach itself to join her gentian train,
you slip down Plato's ladder unashamed.'

THE WEIGHT OF IT

You come out into the floating garden
of early October, there's a mist on your cheek
and you say it's autumn, what have I done

what must I do? and look back at the house
with its cock-eyed face, which you think you want
to leave, but you're seized by a mysterious

invading reverie and stand quite still,
your footprints tracking back in the dew;
the lawn's a mirror where your thought can't settle,

even your language is lost, suddenly
among the grass and the foliage, in the rippling
water of ash leaves against the sky.

And momentarily you're a medium
these presences will trust and pass through
for they know you, and you them,

such has been the constancy of living here;
then the vertigo of time sets in,
as if the years were gathered in an hour

and you're still standing, rooted in the place,
grown into this garden as the garden
has grown into you, a solitary witness

who cannot easily withdraw.
Then you may ask the garden a question:
what is it continuing for,

what kind of certainty can it supply
after the years of watching
and tending? There is no reply.

IN THE COUNTRY

There's no escape this evening
from the silence or the light,

no cover; its intensity slants in
and overruns the old glass
which has wept itself
into pockmarks of distortion.

There's no help for the silhouettes
we've become, looking into rooms
where feelings have run so high
so silently and for so long...

You would turn your back on it
deliberately, at a loss
in front of such a statement,
but early television is flooded out

by its vividness at your back,
its reiteration of beauty,
and behind it stasis and death.

PICARDY

1

Today he named the snow. He is himself
fresh snow, and the baby shoots poking through.

When he looks at the lake
an estuary of light

catches him flush on the face
and borrows his startled breath

to utter itself,
immediate voice, immediate water.

In the musical car
he stares at the winter colours

of Picardy; but the violet scale
and tints of fusco-ferruginous

sill wait to enter his vocabulary.
That in time I shall supply,

for I need him as he needs language;
we're perfect companions for a journey.

2

I can't so easily explain
my thirst for ghosts and expiation

which touches him yet goes beyond
anything I would have him learn;

what makes me drag my toddler round
the whimpering forest of Verdun,

or stand together in a rising mist
on Douaumont, to overlook a battleground

of squalor and obedience.
Trouble closer home has sent me out

to clench myself in a punitive wind
under a bloodshot sky

where I hope to be forgiven
by Our Lady of the Marne

whose infant warns the enemy
Tu n'iras pas plus loin

as my own tugs my sleeve
to bring me away

from this landscape of memorials...

All I would have him learn
are the colours of the field,

mild grey and khaki; the blue horizon.

TRUST

Estranged in a foreign country,
languageless, how I'm here or why

is baffling; it's carpetless and bare
and I am no one. I've come far

from what I haven't thought of
in so long, the absolute safe love

that held me as a child, when home from term
I'd sit beside the fire in my room,

pyjamas warming on a chair.
Tucked up, the last I'd hear

was the firing boiler tremor...
Trust is no less true

than fear,
which comes to look like second nature

yet is not; and nor is dissolution,
for the life's continuous and one

with the child we were
and can recover.

When the jets make loud and clear
that a couple have lost each other

in the machinery of separation,
and I watch the pain

of the man who's left behind,
what comes to mind

is a fashion still from 1938:
careless of the state

in a prospect of war,
a model highkicks on the Eiffel Tower

in a fantail of silliness;
her dancing shoe makes all the impress

of what is personal
on the riveted steel.

And when I witness
the puckered face

of the man left on the ground,
who in a second

will be gone,
driving hard through rain

to loud music, and a drench of tears,
I think of the girl on the bars

and of his girl on the plane,
and the lightness of what is human

is heavier to bear
than the thousands of tons of pressure

which rock the Boeing, as it wobbles
on its cluster of wheels

and skitters forward
with implausible speed

as if, by staying motionless,
it would shake itself to pieces.

FOR PAUL

Paul Le Jéloux, poet, 1955–2015

After a long, disturbed absence,
what I recover from seeing you
is not merely speech, but a pattern
of gestures I loved, the regular slight panic
with which you pat all your pockets in turn
to check on money, cards, cigarettes, lighter –
the debonair way you still brush back your hair,
the efficient unfolding of spectacles…

Maturer? We're older certainly,
greyed, if anything, a touch beyond our years –
warier, not daring, less expectant –
we're not waiting now for any afflatus
or a gladness that came once and not since;
we share a new admiration for serenity
especially when founded on a desolation –
the sober pleasures of the eighteenth century.

But warming to the calvados, the question
at last – *are you writing?* – the creased brow,
sighs, reserve… Soon we're back to the favourites,
the few indispensables for when in need –
romantic, intimate, confessional for the most part –
and the old jokes follow, the latest gossip
on the same old group, and all the savour
being with you has, which is of no date.

PROPHECY

for Myriam

After our ninth separation
I sat in the penitential café

(where a kindly waiter
removed the extra place)

to stupefy myself on wine
and hum *As Time Goes By* too loud

and prepare for the Works of Solitude...
Everyone else was a couple,

leaning over little tables
to mould the face opposite

with fingers and palms...
I knew I would call you up

in a month or so, and saw
the ragged crenellations

of self-sufficiency dissolve
in the immense dilation

you draw
(as into the mystery of my faith)

over your eyes, veil on veil...

AT A GLIMPSE

How often, in Tolstoy,
the cycles of chaos and meaning,
futility and purpose
dejection and joy

hinge on a glimpse of a girl,
a streak of laughter
in yellow, with a black curl
escaping from a kerchief

who is enough to banish
the disabused boredom
the puerile misogyny
the delusion of power

and simply replace them
with herself,
a single high cloud
outlasting the battlesmoke

in the dry eye of Bolkonsky
the wild eye of Rostov
the weak eye of Pierre
the cold eye of Dolohov

before the nihilism
starts again.

VAL DE LOIRE

Cantat philomena sic dulciter...

For nights and days
the aspen poplar
has snowed itself

in fluffy miniature
on the lake and woods;
now, it's white underfoot.

At chosen hours
a pair of buzzard
patrols the treetops

and once a kestrel
mobbed the old grey heron
who turned in outraged circles

and creaked to cover.
At Pentecost
two goldfinch scuffled

upside down on lilac
which has rusted since
and the cherry tree

so garlanded and hooped
was stripped to green
in a day.

The jonquils died,
the tulips died,
the iris died,

and now we have
the generous, unkempt peony,
thornless cousin to the rose

with a scent all her own.
This evening
under a white moon

as daylight lasted
a nightingale uttered
his triplet crescendo

heard by Alcuin
downriver at Saint Martin
in his cell,

where he waited
in retirement
for the knock upon the door;

twelve hundred years
his little bird was rapt
from a spray of broom

beside us, quivering.

TABLET OF THE LAW

Warsaw, 1990

The people's laureate
strides on his podium,
graduate in Collectivism.

Helpmate Wiesława
uplifted stands parallel.
In spanking harness

they plough the end of history
into a republic of play,
the Palace of Culture behind them

much as in *Babar the King*.
He grips a marble tablet
listing the troika

Marx, Engels, Lenin,
and a fourth, struck out.
The blank aches to be filled:

Friedman? Or Loyola.

THE TITANS

for Jerzy Jarniewicz

The city clings to its grime...
Four Titans of Socialist Work
are blacker than most
from implementing the future.

Eyes goggled, ears padded, the men of concrete
are musclebound and cramped
with all their emblems in their arms
bowed beneath a plaster cornice.

On a pristine apron of snow
four bulky moonmen sway and stagger
and stop dead below the stars, drunk
on the weightlessness of a new planet.

ŁÓDŹ

for Anna Tourvas

1

Pedestrian alcoholics
zigzag down the motorway

on the outskirts of Łódź;
there are tractors without tail-lights

and a garish sign
spells *Telimena*, the textile giant

who was once
the aristocratic beauty of Mickiewicz.

I double take the first glimpse
tenements high

made blacker by weak wattage
and cables hanging from housefronts

– it is a gridwork
of unimaginable extension

dissected by a vague arterial
driven through remnants of the ghetto.

There was steam
pouring from every vent and spigot.

2

It was worse than Bleaney's,
the beige flat with green carpeting

salvaged from a very long corridor;
the rooms were a wind tunnel

and the lavatory leaked
above and below.

I went to the *Centrum* for a bite,
was seated at the only unlaid table

in the echoey dining room.
At the far end, a cabaret

was in progress.
A dwarf bicycled on his hands

and a standup comic
shouted like a moustachioed demagogue

at the furniture.
On little plates, acres of egg mayonnaise

stretched away;
and no one came.

3

Nothing could furnish that room,
not my fond mementos,

books, icons, the pocket album
transported wholesale in a trunk.

Simonetta Vespucci
embodies humanist wisdom

but even she, with her coiled hair
and unimpeachable breasts

kept falling from the wall.
Her woman's touch

made no impression
on the uprights of the place.

What remained
was my inert awareness

of decay,
food, skin, paintwork,

and an active neglect,
the deposit of dirt

on my windowsill each morning.

4

The first day, I taught Conrad
or Konrad Korzeniowski

in a windowless amphitheatre
(having groped for a light switch)

to my seminar
of demure beautiful girls.

*And this too has been
one of the dark places of the earth*

– that meant something,

though later they were vexed
by the difficulties

of taking tea at Howards End.

From three o'clock on
at the Grand Hotel…

Down on his luck, a haggard Paderewski
was mixing schmaltz

unheard by free marketeers
consulting over vodka

with the vague criminality
that clings to groups of males

talking too earnestly among themselves.
In the pocket cocktail bar

whores and *gintonic*
were on the agenda;

a German in his cups
bargained through the smoke,

slurping and calling out figures,
raising the stakes

with inflationary abandon
until he hit lucky

and the skinny pomaded teenager
became a radiant smile,

trotted over obediently
and leant her head on his heaving shoulder.

A father walking his little son
between two columns of silver birch

looks immemorial. They're absorbed
in the national pastime

with the courtly shade of Pan Tadeusz
when there was leisure

to name the seven kinds of mushroom
and roll their syllables lovingly on the tongue.

But they disappear and it's like
a pit dug across the path

the forest changes name
to *Waldbezirk 77*

light thickens and dogs
are barking in a ring

at those *goings on*
in grey sealed lorries

ripping in and out
with a tearing of gears.

Sonderbehandlung, like a new
fertiliser, he joked

to the passing forester
who saw him, the jolly policeman,

that weekend,
mushroom picking with his family.

A LETTER FROM AMERICA

for Michael Hofmann

Your letter came from Florida
where you were employed
to produce poets
in the lavish country
of Wallace Stevens.

Your springy students
bounced to ghettoblasters;
they owned convertibles
and spent the afternoon
in surfwear on the beach.

You had a magic haircut
achieved without scissors
and set off the smoke-alarm
by scorching the toast.
Once, in grubby London,

you said you admired
prosperity, your mind
on the German miracle.
Now, in your endearing
practical way

you ask if I have running water
and wonder, with a touch,
perhaps, of envy,
if life is 'abrasive'
in my part of the world.

Well, I did have running water;
when I pulled the bath plug
it ran all over my floor.
I drank vodka,
I queued,

I survived
'my heroic year'
as a Polish colleague put it
with glinting irony.
As a little girl

she lived without knowing it
alongside a people
in a corner of her city
who were encouraged
by Mr Wosk's *Sensational Ideas*

to utilise spoiled potatoes,
to produce ice,
to avoid using glass
in the windows,
and to make the most of coal dust.

from

TRIBUTE

1998

'... *It is My whole Being wrapt up into one Desire, ...*
my Spirit abridged into one perpetual Inclination'

COLERIDGE

PRIMAVERA

Primavera blows across my window,
spring in every language
gusting from the aspen poplar,

flocon, *duvet*, goosedown-gossamer
fluff-clocks in little tourbillons
and whirlpools of the lexicon…

What can I write on her forehead
where the *dolce intelletto d'amore*
has its dwelling, the untranslatable

sweetness and modesty and virtue?
Love stands in memory,
diafan dal lume on a darkness,

flakes of snow-seed blown
into a residue, drifting now
and wasted on the brown, taciturn lake.

HOW WAS THE NIGHT?

after Valéry

How was the night?
At 4, I watched the palm tree
hung with a star.
The extreme calm, the mild
motionless dawn
was infinitely close
to the source of tears,
and the day came slowly
to light up
a store of ruins.
It came to saturate
things that are *all*
ruins in my eyes.

And how was the day?
Fine, golden, absent,
a goddess
I can't believe in anymore.
Despair is a normal,
reasonable state –
the only one that is.
It suppresses
what is yet to be.

Miracle, we say, and destiny,
and joy and hope and repose,

when the one necessary person
lends us fully to ourselves;

and when they've gone, the lengthening light
shows a vista of loss,

proving not that we were wrong –
only the recognition has ruined us.

TRIBUTE

Perilous, this giving over of the self
to your unstable image, my only happiness
uninterrupted contemplation

once the minimum business is done.
It is the struggle for equilibrium
on a tottering rock of meaningless time –

as time has meaning for the saint
only in perpetual adoration.
Around the fact of loss – say it! –

to construct a grammar of recovery
based on untenable articles
and in the teeth of 'good advice':

to praise your flourishing life
from a place in the shadows
will be my comfort and my duty.

THE LAST TIME

I'm exploring the distinction
between *Kronos* and *Kaïros*

and the *durée réelle* that is lived in
only when your tilted eyes are on me.

I'm talking uncontrollably against the time
when you will up and go

vertical with purpose
to leave me stranded

on that iron horizontal
where nothing bears fruit or comes to pass.

A LESSON IN MATERIALISM

Our bedtime book: the letters of Diderot
to Sophie – how he rolled her out a mind –
patient girl – though all I remember now

(was it the same for her?) is the love interest:
we learned to skip the *Encyclopedia*
and came upon that marvellous outburst

of scientific ardour, the great man's prayer,
that when they both should undergo
atomic disaggregation into air

their particles might meet and mingle
in a cloud. We too have undergone
a change; and prematurely single,

tender traces are all I have
(being forced to disassemble you
into everything else that I love).

IDEAL

I had wanted you bodily, your robust frame
anchoring me to the good things of this earth,
but already you are taken from me
by the sun, who hems you with fire, a silhouette
on this deeply shelving dangerous beach,
where you stand out to sea in the breakers:

and what is left me but some droplets
from your salty ringlets shaken out,
and specks of sand fallen back
into uniformity from between your toes,
your castle engulfed already like this island
perhaps we never sailed to.

THE VASE

You wanted to leave flowers
in someone's room.
I was to bring the vase.

You brought wet sprays
of syringa from your garden,
I, an ugly vase.

You brandished your blaze
like a torch, extinguished
by my vase.

You were armfuls of lilies
wilted in the desert
perfected by my vase.

To me you were always
the ideal bouquet,
I the abstract vase.

BLOCKS & SCAFFOLDS

'Paris change! mais rien dans ma mélancolie
N'a bougé!' BAUDELAIRE

for Cécile

This snow on your skin is our duty to the present
falling away on every side at every second
unsharably into avenues estranged from us.

We are elbowed out by the sites and monuments
and the grand promenades of political masters,
captains of industry and moneyed contractors.

Our meagre bundle of human happiness,
or of its opposite, presumably human,
huddles at the foot of a sheer glass precipice.

Machine-washed and replete with cunning light
the crystal pyramid of the cultural state
points up our losses and our own neglect.

You met me in these gardens, a wide smile
in a Russian hat, under trees uprooted since
by the bulldozer of public safety.

These plotted saplings are not for us, my love!
I am the poison tree they carted off to burn
when the city died into traffic and stone.

You were in Rome,
gazing at Bernini's
equivocal angel,
did you recognise
Teresa, stabbed with ecstasy
endlessly?

Ordina questo amore,
O tu che m'ami –
but in the absence
of that order
there is only you
or not you.

Say to the angel of the ossuary
with staring eyes and a finger on her lips,
time heals...
It is a blasphemy;
for she is that tenacious angel
who resurrects unscathed
in the withering sun
and feeds off a diet
of mother's love and youth's perfection.

Say to the lover in his ardent chapel
surrounded by the candlelight
of remorse and propitiation
– perpetuating loss –
(his sickness and distinction)
time heals...
He is burned alive
in the lightning
of a fresh temptation.

BRISEIS

Briseis! *Kallipareos*! by Patroclus led away –
Achilles drawn apart, weeping aloud to the sea –
do we glimpse, at the heart of the quarrel

something more than his wounded pride –
a sense of the unique, the irreplaceable –
my heart's darling – here, a crux – *my wife* –

that is, his slave and concubine? Something, anyway,
dogged Ajax could never understand:
you weep for *one* when we give you *seven*!

Not to mention the twenty Trojan women,
the choice of Agamemnon's daughters
and all those clanking pots and pans to boot!

It isn't manly... Or in the fire of his rhetoric
is it pride become conviction, Briseis mingled
at that moment with the very breath of his life?

True, he goes straight in to lie with Diomede,
also of the matchless cheeks, and there were others,
Helen among them, the dream of everyman.

But true, too, is this: when Achilles weeps with Priam,
Hector dead, and makes the old man comfortable,
and goes inside, there, in his warming bed – Briseis.

Faithful or proud or both, Achilles stands clear –
down in the kingdom of the dead
his longing for life, for any life, unanswerable.

LES FAUX BEAUX JOURS

after Verlaine

All day, the past has fallen
in a hail of flame
ravaging the orange harvest.

It has fastened
on the light-hearted blue
of the singing moment

and sucked you back
to what is gone,
shining in the copper West.

EXTEMPORE

Touching bottom in a provincial station
one hot Sunday of early summer,
the business of meaning stalled

in sunlight on the platform,
my future shunted sideways, a stopped clock,
or a suicide in the hotel bedroom,

I started my life from scratch
sitting on a platform bench,
talking to an affable stranger

with the whiff of drink on his breath
and a carious, defeated smile.
Waiting for my train,

I hung upon his words,
his afternoon of fishing ahead,
followed by a ramble in the woods,

and after that –
I never asked him.
He turned to the sports page, disturbed

by my access of non-sequiturs.
To him, I was unlikely, if not touched,
talking for the sake of it, extempore,

a man from the city, going home,
to a job, family and friends.
Dazed with unbelonging

on the sunny platform,
it seemed I had mistaken him,
and abruptly held my tongue.

QUESTIONS WITHOUT ANSWER

after Montale

People ask me if I've written
a book of love poems
and if my *onlie begetter*
is one or many.
Alas,
my head grows dizzy, so many figures
superimpose themselves
to form a one-and-only, I can barely
make it out in my twilight.
If I had possessed
the obligatory lute
of a sunnier troubadour
it wouldn't be difficult
to name the one who has possessed
my poetical head, or anything else.
If the name
were a consequence of things,
I couldn't name a single one of them,
for things are facts and facts
in perspective are scarcely even ash.
All I had was speech at my disposal,
something that approaches but does not touch;
and there it is –
my heart has no depository
who is not in the grave. That her name
was one name or many does not matter
to him who remains, but a little longer,
outside of divine inexistence. So I say
until then, my ghosts, my adored ones!

SUDDENLY

Suddenly I can walk the streets at peace,
with purpose, not palely loitering.
I can invoke your name among others

without meltdown. You can take your place;
this was, this is, this cannot be undone,
but it can become harmless, just

the memory of a wound
that returns with a pang, but rarely.
I am no longer *waiting*. I could greet you,

and go about my business,
now that I have some business.
We could even reminisce. A breeze!

THE PREMISE

With age there is more in less,
the spring is a work of vacancy,
of milklight through interstices

where the greens go shelving away
in their terraces and towers,
leaving corridors and entrances

breached by the glistening
that issues through them,
the annunciation of nothing

but the flight of birds through space
where space is the premise
we start from and return to, divided

between comfort and dismay.

THE EARTH HIS WITNESS

This spring a single spray
intensifies transparency
and shows the heart of emptiness.

Of all the forms of loss
few are worse
than loss of love by carelessness:

only the random wind
can seem at times to heal
extremities of distress,

or a hand pointing down
touching earth and teaching
the bitter grounds for gladness.

CHAKRA

Give a turn to the wheel, Fortuna,
(sometimes we are stuck head down
too long, noses rubbing along the rut)

– or detach the thing completely,
like this faded spring-green
flywheel I rescued from the nettles,

spoked with an elegant swastika
revolving anticlockwise out of history.
Whatever it turned or was turned by

is broken in pieces. Now it makes
nothing happen. Propped against the wall
it is the symbol of a sermon

that made the world stand still
one day in Sarnath, when the deer knelt down.
It is an obsolete flywheel.

DISCIPLE

That our flowing away
prompts compassion,
I can understand –

that attachment or antipathy
may be undone,
I can understand –

to be equable in all things,
obsessed with none,
I can understand –

that winning or losing
may be as one,
I can understand –

that love's removal
must be begun,
I can understand –

that the emptiness
links everyone –
is difficult.

ABRUPTLY A WING...

Abruptly a wing may open
and come beating
out of the cloudbank

and then a whole
freewheeling company
as if the cloud had stored them

in a long embalming
of ashlight and cumulus:
strangely disinterred

they swoop upriver
in a sequence
of achieved articulations.

CHIMERA

'Une seconde fois perdue!'
NERVAL

Chimeras, firegirls, there's another one now –
blouse Bellini green, a trompe-l'oeil hairgrip
on her chignon, showing a lost domain –
one of your tribe – my familiar, scarecrow,

la guigne stamped on your Russian brow...
No sooner seen, than translated starwards.
She would set you wandering, your orphaned
twin: the prince and princess of sorrow.

Lost and found and lost again – when will it stop?
You were looking elsewhere, at a woodland wraith,
when your chance of happiness married the baker.
My fabulous hairgrip is leaving the shop –

I bequeath her to your legendary worship.
Eyes front, head down, I go my narrow way –
but what if she were *the one?* – I never spoke!
– and so on, and so on, to the end of the rope.

SHCHEGÓL

The goldfinch chatters
beyond himself, ignites
the dreary steppe

of intervening time:
with a bob and a dart
he has come home

to his hole in the laurel,
to his nestmaking business
at the heart

of continuity where he flies,
a flashback of red
in the famished mind.

ARBBRE DE BHONEUR

for Tom

Darling, when you were seven
you wrote with such fluency
about the *arbbre de bhoneur* –
the tassel-haired exotic
we could never identify
outside your bedroom window.

Quand j'ai des chagrin –
all it took to cure you
was the tree of happiness.
Everywhere, the flowers
of consolation were at hand,
morning rose and peony intertwined!

Now you are eleven
and searching for similes
in a copybook exercise –
hence our brainstorming effort
to avoid the cliché
and the wearied rose

when all the impoverishment
of the arbitrary leaves me blank.
On your way to school
the plane trees stand dishonoured,
ugly roadside knuckleheads
shorn of their natural language.

*Mais il y a une chose il faut retenir
c'est un habre de bhonneur...*
And when you come to losing,

that is useful knowledge,
so remember, my darling, your tree,
with its hair *quomme de la neige*.

PUMPKIN

The ruddy-orange pumpkin
is a cry of last colour
in the year;

its empery
is in the stifled plot;
self-seeded,

cephalic and tentacular,
it shows
rudely

through ghostlinen
strung between thistles
in the mulch of neglect.

By a chasm
breached to the West
I carry home

this engorged
harvest of slantlight.
It heats the kitchen

from Michaelmas
to All Souls.
So much for the lantern:

we scoop it hollow
and return it as soup
to the bowl of its gorgeous rind.

HIBERNATION

The colder it gets, the deeper we sleep...
Last night, Pascal's terror
bristled over us
scarified with points of light.

We spared a last thought
for the orbiting spaceman
abandoned out there
whose country no longer exists,

before my lips and teeth
found the soft place,
the mammal's peace,
between your neck and shoulder.

from

YELLOW
STUDIO

2008

IN THE SUN

after Valéry

In the sun on my bed after swimming –
In the sun and in the vast reflection of the sun on the sea,
  Under my window
And in the reflections and the reflections of the reflections
Of the sun and the suns on the sea
  In the mirrors,
After the swim, the coffee, the ideas,
   Naked in the sun on my light-flooded bed
   Naked – alone – mad –
    Me!

RECOGNITION

You were right, righter than you thought, when you asked,
curious at my excess, and *ingénue*,
'Do I remind you of someone?'

Well, yes and no... Something ancient
and new at once, old anima stirring
in her cave, the power of the Name,

calling back through the fields of corn
to Naomi and her daughters, to something
sacred, and I could not answer, instead

there were tears, along with tequilas,
when tilted by a giant hand
I leaned to plant the longest kiss,

as the two phlegmatic zitherers
sat like dummies side by side
and plucked out Zorba's table-dancing kitsch...

After the colour-coding and the blusher
after the Matisse tattoo
after the touch of sprinkle-glitter

(gilding the lily that, if ever)
– there were tears, tears, the true ones, of joy,
(bottle them, bottle them, for later).

Having a Coke with you
            in the *Coffee Parisien*
has got to be more fun
            than trailing to an exhibition
even Picasso's *érotique*;
            and pausing with you by the café
where Pérec wrote
            tentative d'épuisement d'un lieu parisien
is more thrilling
            than *littérature à contraintes*;
I'd rather you took me shopping
            for a pair of two-tone shoes,
and I've never been less in the mood
            and more in need
of decorum
            and a bit of restraint
and of saying less
            and meaning more,
and of everything I preached
            but cannot practise
let alone stretched out with you
            flat on the bookshop floor
with Berryman's *Sonnets*
            'volleying blue air'
because indestructible lightheartedness
            is upon me
whose sweet rare source
            was blindingly there

'I HAVE DREAMED OF YOU SO LONG'

after Desnos

I have dreamed of you so long that you become unreal.

Is there still time to reach your living body and kiss on your mouth the voice that is dear to me where it is born?

I have dreamed of you so long that my arms, crossed against my chest with clasping of your shadow, might not enfold the shape of your body.

So that, in front of the actual appearance of what haunts and compels me for days and years I would surely become a shadow.

O scale-weights of feeling.

I have dreamed of you so long that surely the time for waking has run out. I sleep upright, my body exposed to every appearance of life and love and you, who alone count for me today, I could touch the first lips and the first brow that comes by more than your brow and your lips.

I have dreamed of you so long, walked, talked, slept with your ghost that there may be nothing left for me, but still, to be the ghost among ghosts and one hundred times more shadow than the shadow that moves and shall move gaily over the sundial of your life.

LOVE AND THE NAME

'Like rays from a nucleus, the existence of the loved one proceeds from her name, and even the works created by the lover proceed from the same source.' WALTER BENJAMIN

When I speak the names
they compose a mantra
I have sobbed or murmured
in the night.

The lullaby of their names
neither shortened nor sweetened
is suddenly solemn
like the Aleph or the Om:

the fount of clear water
the saint of music
the golden stone

– names you wear so lightly,
my lost ones, when each
rhymes ecstasy with pain.

ASCENSION DAY

One entire Ascension Day
glued to the earth
hunched against a radiator

reading *La fugitive*
like a fugue, where death
is the theme, *elle ne revint jamais*

as if time could be halted
in the heart of a paragraph, with the entire
giving over of the self

to mourning and desire,
to stasis, to the abolition
of time, her time and mine,

as long as I went on reading, re-reading,
no harm could come
to anyone, nothing could be transformed

and nothing could move on,
or be forgotten,
destroyed, or built upon.

ERMENONVILLE

for Biddy

So it once was, so it is again,
for a single afternoon,

on our bikes, wheels silted up with sand
in the desert of Ermenonville

where the fire girls float their wraiths
at the vague ends of avenues.

They were goblins of melancholy
there among the ferns,

they were sirens, and drove me mad.
This time, for sanity, I pocketed

a pine kernel, to have and to hold,
while you rode ahead

on the path to Mortefontaine
where Corot painted in silver-fleck,

past the well in the road
with its clear-standing water.

This time the eyes were yours
and only yours, sweet tilted,

meeting mine across the years
and your hair *en chignon*, and you straight-backed

and beautiful of carriage
as when I glimpsed you way back when,

papoose strapped in behind you,
cycling decidedly out of my life.

A small field to autumn cyclamen
given up in slantlight, a thicket
of individual lights, the groomed balsam,
the barbed acacia drops her leaves
in a squall, strong weak light, October light,
the precious dregs, the late squibs,
the rapid dripping from the gutter.

A landfall of cloud, brushed up,
blue-violet breasting the Loire,
and the harvest brought down
from the hill, the camber running
reddish and ferment in the vats,
a sour tang, immutable summer
crushed underfoot now, as in *cru*.

LOIRE, AUGUST

Solitude here is not the driven wandering
through a city, but goes deep,
is actually sweet, and is wide as walls
over one yard thick: here a man
can feel the solid chalk beneath his feet,
and wake to the sound of woodpigeons calling
and a light summer rain on the sycamores.
Somewhere down there is the river,
where the terns skim and tumble
threading braids of sand, and fishermen
unchanged since the start of *congés payés*
drop a languid hook, and their womenfolk chat on
in the shade of willows or a white van,
and assorted children fill with their noise
a sunny abeyance: *Les grandes vacances.*

She stalked me
for a year, for a year
I held out, and behold:

a potlatch of toms
sit round her in a ring
with ears pricked

as she rolls among the snowdrops
to rub off his smell
and shows her belly

to urge another on.
She licks the place
and squirms and rolls

what a performance
polite and attentive
the toms wait their turn.

They fled from me
who regard me now
as they might a shadow

a no-man a nothing
no match for them
no match for her, and how

they come around
they come around
the days of oestrus!

And the toms have fucked off
and she mewls at my door
about our future.

CANTO LALAGEN

for Jamie McKendrick

Salve, Lalage

I raise a glass
of the *Roses du Clos*
to where she gathers
her gown at the lawn's end

staring at the god
priapic among birches
she is serene
where now the Diluvian laves her

or else under chafing Dog Star
atrox hora caniculæ
or in the bitter ligerian,
or the riverine damp, she stands

hic in reducta valle
where I left a shears
in the creeper, at the zenith
of a teetering ladder

and only Faunus saved me
from falling to my death
her graces also
interceding

whom now Apollo favours
with slantlight on her belly
and gives since her arrival

a new dispensation

of light and space
guiding and dividing
till all rays lead to her
my *ridens* if not *loquens*

Lalage, *salve!*

METAMORPHOSIS

*Albert Mérat, one of the Vilains Bonshommes, the circle to which
Verlaine and, briefly, Rimbaud belonged, requested that Fantin-Latour
paint him out of the group portrait* Un Coin de Table, *fearing his
reputation would be tarnished.*

Poor Albert Mérat,
le grand Albert,
the elegant, the choleric,
the neurasthenic,
known to his friends as
'the scornful cigar'
met his nemesis
in a baby-faced terror
stalking in from the countryside
with huge hands and huge feet
burning up the foothills
of Young Parnassus.
Genius came at poor Albert
with a sneer and a sword-stick.

He too had his sensitive *Chimères*
praised by *l'oncle Hugo,*
he too had his ode to the anus
censured by Lemerre –
he too his promising beginnings.
He too wore his pen down
and then walked out
of a dreary sinecure.
Wit, wag, *Zutiste à ses heures,*
ladies man, gossip, poet, poseur.
Yet of Albert Mérat
who took fright
nothing is left
but a pot of flowers.

YOUNG MAN

Young man, with a table and a shelf
and Gray's *Anatomy*, setting out
to grasp the trunk of knowledge

and lead the examined life,
perched above the Unjust City
in his nine square metres,

rapt in Spinoza
or moving like an open knife
among the haltered populace

in thrall to its own implacable:
we receive his discourse
as we would the muzzle

of the antlered deer who wanders down
to pluck at the ancient apple-tree
and is so quick to fear.

YELLOW STUDIO

Vuillard's studio, Château des Clayes...
The corner is hard to judge
where the paintings in the painting are pinned
on the yellow wall (the *mise en abyme*
will be the end of me)

in this gleaming Institute of Donors,
this imperial temple
raised from the muck and blood
of the stockyards, out of hog-squeal
and cost-efficient slaughter

at the end of Millennium Park
where the towers crowd and crane
in an ogre's silver egg,
the concentration of capital
in a cunning device.

I stare with nostalgia, with homesickness
into Vuillard's yellow studio
and I know the place
absolutely, it is that humane
heaven of drapes and turpentine

where I shall at last lie down
on the lumpy mattress
with the stripy bedspread
below the little skylight –
my sweet, autarchic rest.

AN ENTHUSIAST

i.m. M.L.R.R. (1927–2001)

Nothing quite dislodged
the early passions, they took possession
hourly, every time my father
walked the marshes, or listened in
to the 'excellent gramophone'
that 'speaks through the wireless'
in his private sitting room,
or weekly without crackle
in the Albert Hall...
Aetat sixteen, he decided
school was loathsome
and nothing mattered anyway
but Music, Ornithology,
a boy called Strode, and God.

Fifty years later
some hardnosed specialist
of consciousness and the genome
held forth at table, claiming
to my father's mild protestation
that Bach's St Matthew Passion
is a product of the human brain
like medicine or the washing machine.
'There is no such thing
as divine inspiration'
and I pushing in
to agree, with an eagerness,
with a vanity,
I now detest and regret.

CORPORAL CONTACT

*'Everything about the ree-lay-shun-ship between men and women
makes me angry. It's all a fucking balls-up. It might have been
organised by the army, or the Ministry of Food.'*
PHILIP LARKIN, JULY 1943

Austerity days
of 'winning the peace',
Churchill growling on the wireless
and my father doing National Service
a little too late for Action
and excused most activity,
asthma confining him to deskwork
amid mass courts-martial
and futile inspections
by the bloody Brass Hats.

A lonesome weekly escapade
out of camp
to the nearest town included
hand-holdings with strangers,
and the girl in front 'rested her lovely head
in my hands'
a voluptuous hour
of 'corporal contact'
during *Brief Encounter*
in the local flea-pit.

Now I have your diary
it is you as well as I
and we act as one
when Brahms's 2nd Piano Conc.
comes on the radio...
I'm still at school
playing it on my Sanyo
Radio-Cassette Recorder,
or escaping my tormentors
in the darkened Music Room,
skulking around the gramophone
illegally, missing Games,
an outcast of the afternoon
wondering what it might be
to 'fit in', and how it might be done,
when the opening horn announces
there must be something more
than this, this is nothing
and I am no one, except for
the savage, dry euphoria
as the piano surges in.

NO INTERRUPTIONS

I cannot wholly decide
about my father's resolve not to speak

or seek out texts
or make arrangements

except perhaps to the pillow
and the blankets.

Was it for him, or for us,
or was he 'in denial'

when he preferred to drift and doze
to music or ambient conversation

as if some unusual act
would make the thing too real?

That adherence to routine,
The Times and the radio, was it

because the stream of time
remained too precious to interrupt early,

as when he waited for the concert to end
before unfolding himself from the car?

FURTHER ENCOUNTERS

The closest we ever were
was a silence facing each other
across the drawing room
in the strict arc of the chairs

Mache dich mein Herze rein
Ich will Jesum selbst begraben

Bach the evangelist ebbed and flowed

and at my back
a crowd of thorns at the window

The two of us rigid unable to speak
or move again least of all
look each other in the eye
I can't remember
who blinked first or why

*

Something of the grey heron
the ashen heron
in your demeanour
when you stood watching herons

– nowhere more so than in that photo
one of the last
where wasting visibly
on that extreme Australian reserve

you took yourself off to
in a further removal
you are standing tall
amongst your leggy waders

*

Leaving the moated lady
who lives where the rivers rise
and where the heron fishes
on the sandbank at the cross-current

I met you on the track in your medium
and nothing could grow old anymore
while the balsam cotton was falling
slowly towards and past me forever

The Peggotty house, upturned wreck,
a caravan-cum-igloo, nursery railway,
a bucket of shingle and drift,
immutable fishermen,
tarred soles, upright sleepers,
the lavateria the common ragwort
where cinnabar caterpillars feed
turning strangely from black and yellow
to black and red and winged;
where he scoured
the ballast pit and the willows for migrants
she hurries through the gorse
through ragwort
and viper's bugloss
the teasels the broom
the purple loosestrife
I name them in trust
the tormentil sweet alison
looking for the lakes
that have wandered, apparently;
and on this anniversary
they haven't heard of him
round here
he has left it all to us,
the nuclear light, the unlikely heat,
the fissures in the carapace,
the brand-new, child-friendly, hands-on Observatory
a short walk from the car-park.

The darling girl
in velvet and satin
who fitted in
so well,

the sweet girl
you kissed
on the doorstep
after the show,

read your secret
loving words
tonight.
That's all I know.

These poems were selected from my four collections, together with a section of 'New Poems' from a fifth. To these I added two translations that first appeared in my anthology *20th-Century French Poems* (Faber, 2002), 'In the Sun' and 'I Have Dreamed of You So Long'.

For some of the historical detail in the Polish poems ('Tablet of the Law' through 'A Letter from America') I am indebted to *The Chronicle of the Łódź Ghetto*, ed. Lucian Dobroszycki (Yale, 1984) and *Łódź Ghetto*, ed. Alan Adelson and Robert Lapides (Viking, 1989).

Grateful acknowledgement is made to the editors of the following journals in which some of the new poems first appeared: *PN Review*, *Poem*, *Spectator*, *Times Literary Supplement*.

'Collects for Lent' appeared in a pamphlet, *Over the Frost* (San Romano, 2016). Five sections of the poem were set to voice, flute and harp by Jeremy Thurlow, first performed at the Prieuré de Lavaray, May 2015. 'Apples' was first published in the *5 Poem* pamphlet series, No. 12 (Clutag Press, 2016).